DEPARTMENT OF THE INTERIOR.
UNITED STATES GEOLOGICAL SURVEY OF THE TERRITORIES.
F. V. HAYDEN, U. S. GEOLOGIST-IN-CHARGE.

THE ELEVATIONS OF CERTAIN DATUM-POINTS ON THE GREAT LAKES AND RIVERS AND IN THE ROCKY MOUNTAINS.

BY

JAMES T. GARDNER, GEOGRAPHER.

[EXTRACTED FROM THE ANNUAL REPORT OF THE UNITED STATES GEOLOGICAL AND GEOGRAPHICAL SURVEY OF THE TERRITORIES FOR 1873.]

WASHINGTON:
GOVERNMENT PRINTING OFFICE.
1875.

1837
ARTES
SCIENTIA
VERITAS
LIBRARY OF THE
UNIVERSITY OF MICHIGAN
E PLURIBUS UNUM
TUEBOR
SI QUAERIS PENINSULAM AMOENAM
CIRCUMSPICE

67

THE ELEVATIONS OF CERTAIN DATUM-POINTS ON THE GREAT LAKES AND RIVERS AND IN THE ROCKY MOUNTAINS.

By James T. Gardner, Geographer.

INTRODUCTION.

As the field of labor of the United States geological and geographical surveys of the Territories now lies in Colorado, the following work was undertaken for the purpose of determining the elevation of Denver, which is at present the base from which all altitudes in the Territory are measured. The height of Denver above the sea had been variously reported at from 5,043 feet to 5,303 feet, and the spirit-level lines of the K. P. and U. P. R. R.s seemed to differ nearly 200 feet. Believing that any such large discrepancies between spirit-level lines must be due to false reports and errors in joining the different links of these long chains to the sea, I determined to reconstruct all possible lines of levels from the ocean to the Rocky Mountains, using only official reports by engineers, and checking them by personal examination of their note-books and working profiles wherever practicable. For this purpose I visited the railroad-engineer offices at Denver, Omaha, Lawrence, Kansas City, Saint Louis, Chicago, Cleveland, New York, and Philadelphia, examining not only the completed profiles and the original notes from which they were made, but making, also, such corrections as then seemed necessary to unite the lines of different companies. Several of the most important profiles were lost in the Chicago fire, and of one of these, that of the C., A., & St. L. R. R., no record is left. Profiles of the C. & N. W. and of the C., R. I., & P. R. R.s had been sent to the geological survey of Iowa, and had been published; these have now to be used instead of the originals.

For many years, various Departments in Washington have been gathering railroad and canal profiles. Mr. Nicholson, the topographer of the Post-Office Department, deserves especial mention for his long-continued activity in this important work under the Smithsonian Institution. Lately, the office of the Chief Signal-Officer of the United States Army has compiled all of this material, with a large collection of their own from original sources, and carefully arranged and indexed it. In the 1871 and 1872 reports of the Chief Signal-Officer, Gen. Albert J. Myer, he speaks of Lieut. Henry Jackson, acting signal-officer and assistant, as having vigorously prosecuted this department of the work. The collection comprises over one thousand profiles and reports from original sources; and efforts are being made to render it so complete, as to the profiles and their connections, that the elevation of every town on railroad or canal shall be well determined. The civil engineers of this country cannot render a greater service to geographical science than to send to the United States Signal-Office copies of railroad and canal profiles. Some of the most important problems in the meteorology of the country are dependent for their solution upon our exact knowledge of the elevations of the observing-stations; and these must be determined independently of the barometer. The elevations should be known to within five feet to satisfy the present needs of meteorology.

The use of this large and admirably-arranged collection was kindly offered me, and to its assistance I am largely indebted for the completeness of this investigation.

The principal difficulties encountered in the present work were: the discrepancies between the different official reports of the profiles of the same railroad or canal; the difficulty of finding the points referred to at the ends of the profiles; the difficulty of connecting them with the mean surface of the ocean; and the clerical errors or mistakes in figures evidently due to copying.

The differences between the reports of the profile of a railroad or canal seem to arise from want of care in computing from the level-notes, and from the fact that they are actually reports of different levelings which do not agree. Generally, a preliminary line of levels is first run over the whole line of the railroad, and bench-marks established; then, when construction is commenced, the different divisions of the line each take one of these bench-marks as the datum for their levels, and build their part of the work from this point. Thus, the line as a whole is really built from many separate datum-planes. Where the different divisions join, they connect their levels so that the relative height of the different datum-planes may be calculated, and all may be reduced to one base. The notes of these connections are generally correct; but, in the first calculations of them, many errors almost always occur, incident upon the hurry and confusion of closing the work and dismissing the engineers for the sake of economy. After the railroad is running, and the chief engineer has leisure to examine the records of his office, errors are found in the calculations of his profiles, and the whole is reviewed and a new profile constructed. It often happens that, after a number of years, either a part or the whole of line is releveled, and a new profile is the result.

Among the profiles which I have examined are representatives of all these classes:

First. Profiles of preliminary lines of survey.

Second. Profiles from first calculation of constructed lines.

Third. Profiles of final calculation of constructed lines.

Fourth. Profiles of final releveling of constructed lines.

Fifth. Profiles made up in the offices by mixing the results of two or more of the above classes.

It is evident that these classes must differ very much in accuracy; and necessarily the first step in this examination was to determine upon methods of testing the profiles so as to fix their proper relative weights. This was a very complicated and difficult process on account of the number of factors to be considered. Some of the principles may, however, be stated.

If two points were connected by several independent lines of railroad or canal, the agreement of these lines as to the difference of altitude of the termini was considered one of the best tests of accuracy.

If one of these lines was a canal which had been releveled many times, and the termini carefully connected with the other lines, and of which we had a final official report, this was taken as true and used as a standard of comparison for the accuracy of the other lines.

If the lines were all canal-levels, their relative weight was determined by the number of times they had been releveled, the recentness of the work, the recentness of the official report, and its detailed character.

If the lines were all railroad-levels, the following points were considered as favorable to the character of any line or connection of lines:

First. That the official reports should be recent and detailed.

Second. That they should be reports of the final computation of the construction-levels, or a releveling of the completed line, or, best of all, that we should have both of these reports agreeing closely.

Third. That there should be few connections of lines formerly independent to make up the present through-line.

Fourth. That, where the line was made up by joining several parts formerly independent, the connection between them should not be open to any doubt.

If, of several lines between two points, one disagreed largely from the others of apparent equal weight, it was considered as probably in error.

If several railroads, running from a common point, cross an important river, the fall of the stream was determined by the very best lines, and those were rejected which made it run up hill or gave an improbable fall.

If several parallel railroads were cut by a cross-line, well connected, their agreement upon this common line was considered as an important test.

If several lines of levels between two points start from a common datum or directrix, and end also at a common datum, the connection for comparison is far more reliable than when the ends of the lines merely came into the same city, and then have to be joined by connecting the depots by city-levels.

The results of the application of these standards of accuracy showed that recent official reports of the final computation of the construction-levels were generally reliable so far as any one line is concerned. The Pa. R. R. may be given as one of the best examples. It has been recently releveled, and though there was a discrepancy between the new and old elevations of Pittsburgh of 11 feet, it was found on a third leveling of a part of the line that this was due to erroneous connection of two leveling-parties, and all occurred at one point. And now, when a final computation of the old construction-levels, and of the new and corrected line, is made, the elevation of Pittsburgh by the new line is within a foot of the old. Great credit is due to Mr. Wilson, the consulting engineer of this road, for the interest he has taken in investigating the discrepancies of the Pa. R. R. profiles, and through his exertions we have at last a correct report of the profile of that important railroad so many years after the levels were run. The profiles that seemed from their dates to be first calculations of constructed lines were often found unreliable, and do not generally agree with the final calculation of the levels when we have reports of both. The profiles of preliminary lines of survey were, of course, found very unreliable. The elevations of Cairo, Ill., and Columbus, Ky., have hitherto rested on a preliminary survey of the M. & O. R. R. from Mobile Bay, and seem to be 10 to 15 feet below the better determinations.

The worst of all the profiles, and the most perplexing to the geographer, are those made up in the offices of some of the railroads by putting together data from old and new printed reports and from all the manuscript profiles in the office, and treating them as if the same datum of levels was referred to in all these sources of information. The mixture thus produced generally defies the most ingenious power of analysis in the searcher after truth.

In general, I am satisfied that *the important errors in our railroad and canal profiles are not so much due to imperfect instrumental work as to hasty computation and careless combination of the results.*

The difficulties of making connection between the end of one profile and the beginning of another have been very great. Most cities have now a datum or base-point from which all the city-levels date, often called the city directrix. The United States Signal-Office has taken great pains to get reports from most of the city-engineers of the heights of the railroad-depots above these city-directrices; but the difficulties of using this connection between railroads is that in many cases the present depots are not the ones referred to on the profiles of the roads; and even when the present depots are the same as the old ones, the grade at the depot has been changed since the railroad-profile was made, and no note of the present grade made on the profile. This seems to be the case in Chicago, where the railroad-profiles almost all indicate a lower grade for the depots than those reported by the city-engineer.

By visiting the ground, and making connections with old benches, I have gotten rid of many of these errors, and, fortunately, in many cities the railroad-engineers have connected their datum with that of the city. If the engineers of this country will adopt this as a rule, the value of their work for general and scientific purposes will be very much increased.

The railroad-lines from Philadelphia, and the railroad and canal lines from Albany, had reported the elevations along their lines above tides of various stages at these points, and the G. T. R. W. of Ca. had reported their elevations as referred to tide at Three Rivers, the head of tide-water in the Saint Lawrence. These datum-points differ from each other, and from the mean surface of the ocean, which is the only proper plane of reference for our elevations. The errors due to this cause have entered into all previous reports of elevations in Pennsylvania and the regions about the great lakes. By the assistance of the United States Coast Survey, and of Mr. Smedley, city engineer and surveyor of Philadelphia, the datum-planes of the Erie Canal and N. Y. C. R. R. levels and of the Pa. R. R. have been connected with the mean surface of the ocean.

Important changes are made as the result of this investigation. The elevation of the great lakes and surrounding country is found to be about 9 feet more than previously reported by the State geologist of Ohio, and that of Saint Louis about 23 feet higher than reported by Humphreys and Abbot. While Kansas City, and all the surrounding country for many hundred miles south and west, has heretofore been reported more than 100 feet too low, Omaha is raised about 31 feet, and Indianapolis about 100 feet. The fall of the Mississippi above Memphis, and of the Ohio, and of the Missouri River, is also changed. The amounts of these changes are so great, and the accuracy of the results of such importance to science and to our work of internal improvements, that I publish the evidence upon which they rest, and a statement of the evidence upon which previous reports were made where such could be found.

The checking at Denver of the levels brought through by the U. P. and D. P. R. R., and by the K. P. R. R. is so close that I believe the error of elevation of this point cannot exceed 10 feet, exclusive of that due to deflection of the plumb-line by attraction of mountain-masses. The result by the K. P. R. R. is 5198.97; and by the U. P. and D. P. R. R.s, 5194.20 feet above mean sea. My determinations of the elevation of Ogden, above the Atlantic Ocean, by the U. P. R. R., and above the Pacific Ocean, by the C. P. R. R., differ only 25 feet. When it is considered that the line of levels from the Atlantic to Ogden, Utah, is about two thousand miles long, this discrepancy is small. It is not improbable that a large part of this error lies between Cheyenne and Ogden, where the work on the U. P. R. R. was driven at an unprecedented speed, and where the line lies over mountains. The accompanying map shows the lines of levels that have entered into this discussion.

Discussion of evidence of the altitudes of various points in the United States and Canada.

THE ELEVATION OF LAKE ONTARIO.

	Feet.	Various datum-planes.	Elevation in feet above mean surface of Atlantic Ocean.
First determination.			
Mean tide at Albany, by United States Coast Survey leveling.	4.84	Above mean tide west end of Eighteenth street, New York.	4.84
Mean surface of Lake Ontario, by report of final levelings of Erie Canal, (see profiles accompanying annual report of State engineer and surveyor of New York, January 1, 1868. by J. P. Goodsell.)	245.15	Above M. T., Albany	....
Mean surface of Lake Ontario	....	....	249.99
Second determination.			
Mean tide in St. Lawrence River at Three Rivers, datum of levels of G. T. R. W. of Canada.	6.77	Above M. H. T., at Portland, Me.	....
Surface of Lake Ontario	235.00	Above M. T., Three Rivers.	....
Do	241.77	Above M. H. T., Portland	....
(These figures are from a report of the chief engineer of the G. T. R. W. of Canada, dated March. 1872.)			
Mean high-tide at Portland, Me., by United States Coast Survey report.	4.5	Above M. T., Portland..	....
Surface of Lake Ontario	....	....	246 27
Final results.			
Surface of Lake Ontario:			
First determination	....	....	249.99
Second determination	....	....	246.27
Adopted as correct	....	....	249.99
Error of second determination	− 3.72	....	....

The first determination is adopted, because it is the final result of many years' leveling over the line of the Erie Canal, as against the result of a long and broken line of railroad-levels; and because the canal-engineers have undoubtedly taken greater pains to get the mean surface of the lake than the railroad-engineers, to whom such knowledge was of no practical importance.

At Montreal, the levels of the G. T. R. W. are checked approximately by levels run by the Montreal and Champlain R. R. Co., Montreal, summer, water in river is 30 feet above mean sea by the G. T. R. W.; by the M. & C. levels L. W. at Montreal is 69.7 feet below L. W. Champlain. The surface of the lake is 100.84 feet by canal from Albany; hence L. W. Montreal about 31 feet. Considered with reference to Lake Champlain, we have its height above mean sea 100.84 feet by Hudson River and Whitehall Canal, and 99.7 feet by G. T. R. W. from Portland.

ELEVATION OF BUFFALO, CLEVELAND DIRECTRIX, AND MEAN SURFACE OF LAKE ERIE.

	Feet.	Various datum-planes.	Elevation in feet above mean surface of Atlantic Ocean.
First determination.			
Mean tide at Albany, N. Y., by United States Coast Survey leveling.	4.84	Above M. T. foot of Eighteenth street, New York.	....
Surface of water in Erie Canal at Buffalo, by report of final levelings of Erie Canal, (see profiles accompanying annual report of State engineer and surveyor of New York, January 1, 1868, by J. P. Goodsell.)	568.42	Above M. T. Albany	....
Water-prism of this section 9 feet deep; hence, bottom of canal at Buffalo.	559.42	......do	....
Surface of Erie Canal, Buffalo	....	....	573.26
Bottom of Erie Canal, Buffalo	....	....	564.26
Surface of Lake Erie, by observations at Cleveland and Buffalo from 1844 to 1857, and published in Smithsonian Contributions, by C. Whittlesey, 1860.	8.82	Above bottom of Erie Canal.	....
Mean surface of Lake Erie at Buffalo	568.24	Above M. T. Albany	....
Do	....	....	573.08
Cleveland directrix, by mean of a very favorable month of synchronous observations at Buffalo and Cleveland on surface of lake, by Mr. C. Whittlesey and Mr. J. Lathrop.	11.42	Above bottom of Erie Canal, Buffalo.	....
Cleveland directrix	....	....	575.68
Do	2.60	Above M. S. of Lake Erie from 1844 to 1857.	....
Mean surface of Lake Erie from 1844 to 1857	....	....	573.08
Second determination.			
Permanent United States Coast Survey bench on granite block at Gloucester Ferry, N. J., by United States Coast Survey Report of 1871.	8.10	Above M. T. Raritan Bay, equal mean surface of Atlantic.	....
Mean tide in Delaware River at Philadelphia, by United States Coast Survey Report.	4.751	Below U. S. C. S. bench	....
Mean tide at Philadelphia	....	....	3.349
Philadelphia city datum, by leveling of Mr. S. L. Smedley, city-engineer and surveyor, and his assistant, Mr. Herring, January 11, 1874.	0.632	Above U. S. C. S. bench	....
Philadelphia city datum	....	....	8.732
Pennsylvania R. R. datum, by report of Mr. Wilson, consulting-engineer of P. R. R., 1874.	1.819	Below Philadelphia city datum.	....
Pennsylvania R. R. datum or base of levels, called H. T. at Philadelphia.	....	....	6.913
Harrisburgh, Market street depot track	313.00	Above P. R. R. datum	....
Do	....	....	319.913
Pittsburgh, Union depot track	738.00	Above P. R. R. datum	....
Do	....	....	744.913
(The above elevations are from a profile of the last computations from releveling the whole line, agreeing within one foot with the old construction-levels at Pittsburgh. Report by Mr. Wilson, consulting-engineer, April 29, 1874.)			
Alliance, by P. F. W. & C. R. R. profile, 1872	336.70	Above Union depot, Pittsburgh.	....
Alliance, (track)	....	....	1,081.613
Cleveland directrix, by profile of C. & P. R. R., reported by Mr. I. Pillsbury, February 11, 1858.	507.55	Below Alliance	....
Cleveland directrix	....	....	574.063
Crestline, (track,) by profile of P. F. W. & C. R. R.	407.60	Above Union depot, Pittsburgh.	....
Crestline	....	....	1,152.51
Cleveland directrix, by profile of C. C. C. & I. R. R., reported by Mr. I. Pillsbury, February 11, 1858.	577.30	Below Crestline	....
Cleveland directrix	....	....	575.21
Cleveland directrix, mean of Crestline and Alliance routes.	....	....	574.637
Mean surface of Lake Erie	....	....	572.037
Third determination.			
Mean tide Albany, by United States Coast Survey	4.84	Above M. T. New York ..	....
Buffalo, N. Y. C. & L. S. R. R. depot track, by profile of N. Y. C. R. R.	578.23	Above tide at Albany, assumed to be M. T.	....
Buffalo, N. Y. C. depot track	....	....	583.07

Elevation of Buffalo, Cleveland directrix, and mean surface of Lake Erie—Continued.

	Feet.	Various datum-planes.	Elevation in feet above mean surface of Atlantic Ocean.
Third determination—Continued.			
Cleveland, L. S. depot track, by profile of L. S. & M. S. R. R.	0. 70	Above Buffalo depot track.	....
Cleveland, L. S. R. R. depot track	....	....	583. 77
Cleveland, L. S. R. R. depot track, by city-engineer report.	8. 5	Above city-directrix	....
Cleveland directrix	....	....	575. 27
Mean surface of Lake Erie	....	....	572. 67
Fourth determination.			
Junction of the N. C. & Pa. R. Rs., on main line of Pa. R. R., west of Harrisburgh, by profile of N.C.R.R.	350. 00	Above M. T. Baltimore	....
Harrisburgh, Market street depot track	30. 25	Below junction of N. C.	....
Do	....	....	319. 75
Surface of Lake Erie, (year not given,) by P. & E. R. R.	251. 00	Above Harrisburgh	....
Surface of Lake Erie, (year unknown)	....	....	570. 75
Fifth determination.			
Erie Railway depot at Dunkirk	606. 80	Above M. T. New York	....
Surface of Lake Erie at Dunkirk, by profile supposed to be from construction-levels.	582. 20	......do	....
(The present chief engineer reports that the line has been rerun, and that the old and new lines differ over 20 feet in some places. After examining the old and new levels, he gives preference to the old, but considers both incorrect.)			
Cleveland, L. S. depot, by L. S. & M. S. R. R	14. 5	Below Dunkirk	....
City directrix	8. 5	Below Cleveland depot	....
Cleveland directrix	23. 00	Below Dunkirk	....
Do	....	....	583. 80
Mean surface of Lake Erie	....	....	581. 20
(This result is rejected in making up the means, because the levels are condemned by the chief engineer of the road.)			
Sixth determination.			
Surface of Lake Ontario, by G. T. R. W. of Canada	....	....	246. 27
Surface of water in Detroit River opposite Detroit, by G. W. R. W. of Canada.	328. 40	Above mean surface of Lake Ontario.	....
Surface of Lake Erie by State geological survey report.	3. 00	Below river at Detroit	....
Surface of Lake Erie	....	....	571. 67
Final results.			
Lake Erie:			
First determination	....	Mean surface	573. 08
Second determination	....	......do	572. 037
Third determination	....	......do	572. 670
Fourth determination	....	......do	570. 750
Fifth determination	....	......do	[581. 20]
Sixth determination	....	......do	571. 67
Adopted result.			
Surface of Lake Erie, mean of observations from 1844 to 1857.	....	....	573. 08
Differences of other results from the one adopted.			
Second determination differs	− 1. 04	....	....
Third determination differs	− 0. 41	....	....
Fourth determination differs	− 2. 33	Year unknown	....
Sixth determination differs	− 1. 41	......do	....
(The first determination is adopted, because it is the final result of many years' leveling on the Erie Canal, connected with the mean of thirteen years' observations on the surface of the lake.)			
Cleveland directrix:			
First determination	....	....	575. 68
Second determination	....	....	574. 637
Third determination	....	....	575. 270

Elevation of Buffalo, Cleveland directrix, and mean surface of Lake Erie—Continued.

	Feet.	Various datum-planes.	Elevation in feet above mean surface of Atlantic Ocean.
Adopted result.			
Cleveland directrix, (this is high-water mark of 1838 on pier.)	....	....	575.68
Differences of the other results from the one adopted.			
Second determination differs	− 1.04	....	....
Third determination differs	− 0.41	....	....

The first determination is adopted, because it is the result of many years' leveling over the Erie Canal, connected with Cleveland by a very favorable month of observations on the lake surface, and connected with mean sea by the levels of the United States Coast Survey.

The United States Coast-Survey line from their tide-gauge at New York to that at Albany was run for scientific purposes, and is undoubtedly leveling of the first quality. The Erie Canal has been in process of construction and enlargement for over fifty years. During this time the levels must have been rerun many times, and the benches and computations checked by a succession of different engineers. Their final report should be of the highest authority. The mean surface of Lake Erie, during a month with light winds, when the fluctuations of the lake were small, is considered a level plane for connecting the west end of the canal with Cleveland. I think these reasons sufficient to justify me in accepting the first determination as against those by the railroad-lines.

The result may then be considered as showing great accuracy in the railroad surveys, which are from 480 to 600 miles long, and yet differ but about one foot from the canal-levels.

At Harrisburgh, where the lines of the second and fourth determinations cross, the checking is very close. The height, as brought by the U. S. C. S. and Pa. R. R. from Raritan Bay, one hundred and seventy-five miles, is 319.91, while that brought from Baltimore by the N. C. R. R. is 319.75; the two differing only $\frac{16}{100}$ of a foot. The elevation of this same Market-street depot at Harrisburgh by the P. & R. R. R., reported to me by the chief engineer May, 1874, is 308.03 above M. T. Philadelphia, which would be 311.38 above M. T. Atlantic Ocean. This line is evidently in error about 8 feet betwe n Philadelphia and Harrisburgh, but I believe it to be mostly in their computation, and not in the instrumental work.

At Pittsburgh the Pa. R. R. is again checked by the B. & O. R. R., which, in a number of reports, give the elevation of their depot as 735 feet above mean tide at Baltimore. By the report of the city-engineer, the B. & O. R. R. depot track is 7.75 feet below that of the Union depot; hence the elevation of the track in the Union depot at Pittsburgh, by the B. & O. R. R. above M. T. Baltimore, is 742.75 feet. That by the Pa. R. R. was 744.91 feet above M. T. Raritan Bay. As it is not known to me how this mean tide was determined at Baltimore, nor is it known whether mean tide at Baltimore is the same as the mean ocean-surface, and as the B. & O. R. R. levels have not been subject to as many revisions as those of the Pa. R. R., and the connection of the Pittsburgh depot is not known to be with the same grade given in the profiles of the railroad, I consider the Pa. R. R. result as being the more reliable for the present elevation of the track in the Union depot.

The line of levels from Baltimore, by the N. C. R. R. to Harrisburgh, and thence, by the P. & E. R. R. to Lake Erie, at Erie, a distance of four hundred and twenty-six miles, reaches the lake with an error that does not exceed 2 feet.

ELEVATIONS OF LAKE HURON, LAKE MICHIGAN, AND THE CHICAGO DIRECTRIX.

	Feet.	Various datum-planes.	Elevation in feet above mean surface of Atlantic Ocean.
First determination.			
Lake Ontario at Oswego, by United States Coast Survey and Erie Canal.	....	....	249.99
Surface of Georgian Bay, Lake Huron, at Collingwood, by N. R. R. of Canada.	340.00	Above Lake Ontario......	....
Surface of Lake Huron in Georgian Bay........	....	....	589.99
Second determination.			
Surface of Lake Huron at Sarnia, south end of lake, by G. T. R. W. of Canada.	341.00	Above Lake Ontario......	....
Surface of Lake Huron........	....	....	590.99
Third determination.			
Mean surface of Lake Huron at Sarnia, by G. W. R. W. of Canada.	340.00	Above Lake Ontario.....	....
Mean surface of Lake Huron........	....	....	589.99
Fourth determination.			
Mean surface of Lake Erie, by United States Coast Survey and Erie Canal.	....	....	573.08
Surface of Detroit River at Detroit, by State geological survey report.	3.00	Above Lake Erie	....
Mean Surface of Lake Huron, by G. W. R. W. of Canada.	11.60	Above surface of river at Detroit.	....
Difference of Lake Erie and Lake Huron, mean surfaces.	14.60	....	....
Mean surface of Lake Huron........	....	....	587.68
Fifth determination.			
Surface of Detroit River at Detroit, by State geological survey report.	3.00	Above Lake Erie.	....
Junction of D. & M. R. R. and G. T. R. R., by D. & M. R. R.	55.60	Above water in Detroit River, Sept. 24, 1868.	....
Surface of Lake Huron, by G. T. R. W. of Canada	43.00	Below Milwaukee junction	....
Lake Huron........	12.6	Above river at Detroit, September 24, 1868.	....
Do	15.6	Above Lake Erie........	....
Surface of Lake Huron........	....	....	588.68
Sixth determination.			
Surface of Detroit River at Detroit........	3.00	Above Lake Erie........	....
Surface of Lake Michigan at Grand Haven, by D. & M. R. R.	10.74	Above river at Detroit, September 24, 1868.	....
Lake Michigan........	13.74	Above Lake Erie........	....
Surface of Lake Michigan........	....	....	586.82
Seventh determination.			
Cleveland directrix........	....	....	575.68
Crestline, by C. C. C. & I. R. R	577.30	Above Cleveland directrix.	....
Crestline	....	....	1,152.98
Chicago depot of P. F. W. & C. R. R. track, by P. F. W. & C. R. R. report, 1872.	558.6	Below Crestline........	....
Chicago, P. F. W. & C. depot track	....	....	594.38
Chicago city directrix, by city-engineer, 1872........	8.5	Below top of rail in P. F. W. & C. depot.	....
Chicago directrix........	....	....	585.88
Mean surface of Lake Michigan for past twenty years, by city-engineer's report.	2.00	Above city-directrix......	....

ELEVATIONS OF LAKE HURON, ETC.—Continued.

	Feet.	Various datum-planes.	Elevation in feet above mean surface of Atlantic Ocean.
Surface of Lake Michigan, mean of twenty years			587.88
Alliance, by C. & P. R. R	507.55	Above Cleveland directrix	
Alliance			1,083.23
Chicago depot, track of P. F. W. & C. R. R., by P. F. W. & C., 1872, report.	487.7	Below Alliance	
Chicago depot, track P. F. W. & C. R. R			595.53
Chicago directrix, by city-engineers, 1872	8.50	Below depot track	
Chicago directrix			587.03
Surface of Lake Michigan, mean of past twenty years			589.03
Chicago directrix, by P. F. W. &. C. R. R., mean of Alliance and Crestline connection with Cleveland.			586.46
Surface of Lake Michigan			588.46
Eighth determination.			
Cleveland directrix			575.68
Cleveland, L. S. & M. S. depot, by city-engineer	8.50	Above directrix	
Chicago, L. S. & M. S. depot track, by profile procured at the office of chief engineer, October, 1873.	16.6	Above Cleveland depot	
Chicago, L. S. & M. S. R. R. depot track			600.78
Chicago directrix, by city-engineer, 1872	12.80	Below track of L. S. & M. S. depot.	
Chicago directrix			587.98
Surface of Lake Michigan, mean of past twenty years			589.98
Ninth determination.			
Mean surface of Lake Erie			573.08
Mean surface of river at Detroit, by State geological survey report.	3.00	Above Lake Erie	
Usual height of water in river on June 1	1.00	Above mean surface of river.	
Chicago depot of M. C. R. R., by M. C. R. R. report	13.20	Above river at Detroit, June 1, 1869.	
Chicago depot of M. C. R. R. & I. C. R. R			590.28
Chicago directrix, by chief engineer of I. C. R. R	6.5	Below I. C. & M. C. R. R. depot.	
Chicago directrix			583.78
Mean surface of Lake Michigan			585.78
Final results.			
Surface of Lake Michigan and Lake Huron:			
(2) First determination	Huron	State of water unknown	589.99
(2) Second determination	..do	......do	590.99
(2) Third determination	..do	Mean surface	589.99
(1) Fourth determination	..do	......do	587.68
(1) Fifth determination	..do	State of water unknown	588.68
(1) Sixth determination	Michigan	......do	586.82
(4) Seventh determination	..do	Mean surface	588.46
(4) Eighth determination	..do	......do	589.98
(1) Ninth determination	Michigan	......do	585.78
(The figures in parentheses indicate the relative weights with which the different determinations enter into the mean.)			
Adopted result.			
Mean of nine determinations			589.15
Mean surface of Lake Michigan for past twenty years			589.15
The extreme range among the nine results is	4.21		
(This amount does not exceed the known fluctuations of the lakes.)			
Chicago directrix:			
Seventh determination			586.46
Eighth determination			587.98
Mean			587.22
Result by subtracting 2 feet from adopted result for mean surface of the lake.			587.15
Adopted result.			
Chicago city-directrix			587.15
The observations at Chicago make the city-directrix	2.00	Below mean surface of Lake Michigan for past twenty years.	

Hence, if the height 589.15 feet is adopted as the mean surface, 587.15 feet must be the elevation of the city-directrix. I have given their respective relative weights to the different determinations for the following reason: The fourth, fifth, sixth, and ninth are of least value, because they depend on the height of the water at Detroit, being 3 feet above Lake Erie, as reported by the State geological survey. The original data upon which this report depends cannot be found, and I therefore consider it open to much doubt. The first, second, and third determinations are given the value (2) because they are first-class railroad-lines, run from a base at Toronto, called surface of Lake Ontario, but which I do not *know* to be the mean surface, but simply *assume* it to be so. They run directly to Lake Huron, but only in one case is the state of the water given; and then I do not know of how many years it is the mean. These results should, of course, be far better than the fourth, fifth, sixth, and ninth, but are not nearly so probable as the seventh and eighth, which depend on railroad-lines run directly from the Cleveland directrix to the Chicago depots, which in this case seem well connected with the Chicago directrix. The height of the Cleveland directrix, as brought through on these same railroad-lines, the L. S. & M. S., the P. F. W. & C., C. & P., and C. C. C. & I. R. Rs. had checked so closely with the canal and lake surface result that they are entitled to great weight in their westward extension to Chicago. In connection with these directrices of Cleveland and Chicago, the fluctuations of the lakes have been observed, and the mean surfaces determined. For accounts of these fluctuations see Smithsonian Contributions, 1860: Fluctuations of Level in the North American Lakes, by Charles Whittlesey; also a recent report from the Dudley observatory, Albany, N. Y.

Determinations 1, 2, 3, 7, and 8 are the only ones which rest upon sufficient evidence to make them of much value, and it will be noticed that the range among these five is only 2.53 feet, with the lake at an unknown stage of the water. The range among those three that refer to the mean surface of Lakes Huron and Michigan is only 1.53 feet. I think therefore that the elevations of the mean surface of Lake Michigan and of the Chicago directrix will probably not be open to a change of over one foot. We have here at the Chicago directrix an opportunity for comparing the results of two very long and independent lines of railroad-levels, those of the N. Y. C. and L. S. & M. S. R. Rs., and of the Pa. R. R. and P. F. W. & C. R. R. I give the results in detail:

From mean tide New York Bay to the Chicago directrix.

	Feet.	Various datum-planes.	Elevation in feet above mean surface of Atlantic Ocean.
By the N. Y. C. R. R.:			
Mean tide Albany, by United States Coast Survey.	4. 84	Above M. T. New York ..	....
Buffalo depot, by N. Y. C. R. R.	578. 23	Above T. at Albany	....
Chicago depot, by L. S. & M. S. R. R	17. 30	Above Buffalo depot......	....
Chicago directrix....	12. 80	Below Chicago, L. S. & M. S. depot.	....
Do	....	....	587. 57
Total distance from New York Bay, 980 miles.			
By the Pa. R. R.:			
Pa. R. R. datum, by United States Coast Survey..	6. 913	Above M. T. Raritan Bay.	....
Pittsburgh Union depot, by Pa. R. R..............	738. 00	Above Pa. R. R. datum....	....
Chicago depot, by P. F. W. & C. R. R	151. 00	Below Pittsburgh depot ..	....
Chicago directrix..................................	8. 50	Below Chicago depot......	....
Do	....	....	585. 41
Total distance, about 900 miles.			
Chicago directrix, by N. Y. C. & L. S. & M. S. R. R., 980 miles.	587. 57	Above M. T. New York...	....
Chicago directrix, by Pa. R. R. & P. F. W. & C. R. R., 900 miles.	585. 41	Above M. T. Raritan Bay	....
Difference..	2. 16	....	....

These lines are about one hundred and fifty miles apart through the first half of their course and about fifty miles in the western part. The Pa. R. R. crosses the Appalachian-mountain system in a difficult place, rising to a height of 2,290 feet, among ridges that must exert considerable attraction upon the level, while the N. Y. C. and L. S. & M. S. Railroads are through comparatively level country; and yet, after this long course of about nine hundred miles, they reach Chicago with only two feet difference in their levels. The result seems truly remarkable. The height by the Pa. R. R. differs—1.74 feet, and by the N. Y. C., L. S. & M. S. R. R. +0.42 feet from the adopted elevation.

The N. Y. C. R. R. is checked at Buffalo, three hundred miles from Albany, by a connection with surface of Lake Erie, state of water unknown, but assumed to be mean surface. The railroad-levels are 0.7 foot too high. At Cleveland, four hundred and eighty miles from Albany, the railroad-levels are 0.41 feet too high, and at Chicago 0.42 feet too high. The Pa. R. R. is checked at Harrisburgh, one hundred miles from Philadelphia, where it is intersected by the N. C. R. R., bringing its levels from mean tide at Baltimore, eighty-four miles. The two lines of levels differ but 0.16 feet. It is checked again at Pittsburgh, three hundred and fifty miles from Philadelphia, where the B. & O. R. R. intersects, bringing its levels from mean tide at Baltimore about three hundred miles. The levels by the Pa. R. R. are 2.16 feet higher than by the B. & O. R. R., but the connection of the profiles of the two is not exactly certain. It is, however, not improbable that mean tide at Baltimore is a little above the mean level of the ocean. At Alliance, the P. F. W. & C., the extension of the Pa. R. R. line of levels to Chicago, is checked by the C. & P. R. R. from the Cleveland directrix. The elevation of Alliance by the Pa. R. R. and P. F. W. & C. R. R. is 1081.61 feet; that by the C. & P. R. R. is 1083.23 feet; the P. F. W. & C. being probably too low.

At Crestline it is checked again from the Cleveland directrix, the elevation by the P. F. W. & C. R. R. being 1152.51, and that by the C.

C. C. & I. R. R. 1152.98; the P. F. W. & C. being probably too low. At Chicago, the P. F. W. & C. R. R. levels are 1.74 feet too low. The mean of these checks at Alliance, Crestline, and Chicago would make the whole of the western part of this line 1.27 feet too low. I therefore think it not improbable that the elevation of Pittsburgh by the Pa. R. R. may be about 1 foot too low. Considering all the evidence, I should be inclined to adopt 746 feet as the elevation of Pittsburgh Union-depot track instead of the Pa. R. R. result of 744.913.

The longest connected line of railroad-levels that we have an opportunity to check at Chicago is that of the G. T. R. W. of Canada, from Portland, Me., to Detroit, Mich., and thence to Chicago by the M. C. R. R. The details of the line and its results are as follows:

Elevation of Chicago directrix by G. T. R. W. of Canada and M. C. R. R.

	Feet.	Various datum-planes.	Elevation in feet above mean surface of Atlantic Ocean.
Mean high tide at Portland	4. 5	Above M. T. Portland	
Mean tide, G. T. R. R. datum at Three Rivers	6. 77	Above M. H. T. Portland	
Toronto	239. 78	Above G. T. R. W. datum	
Detroit junction	340. 22	Above Toronto	
Chicago depot	4. 70	Below Detroit junction	
Chicago directrix	6. 50	Below depot of M. C. R. R	
Do			580. 07
Distance from Portland to Chicago 1,142 miles.			

My adopted elevation is 587.15 feet; therefore, this line of levels, eleven hundred and forty-two miles long, appears to be in error only 7.08 feet, and the greater part of this error is in the M. C. R. R. line in the last three hundred miles. The quality of the line in different parts is shown by the checks at various points. The first check is at Toronto, six hundred and thirty miles from Portland, where the line is connected with the surface of Lake Ontario, the state of the water unknown, but assuming it to be the mean surface, the levels are 3.72 feet too low. The next check is at Sarnia, on Lake Huron, eight hundred miles from Portland, where the line is connected with the surface of this lake; the state of the water is again unknown, but, if assumed it to be the mean surface, the levels are 1.88 feet too low. At Detroit junction we have an approximate check by the height of that point, by the M. C. R. R., above H. W. in river at Detroit, June 1, 1869. The M. C. R. R. gives the height of Grand Trunk junction at 17.90 feet above H. W. 1869. This point we have supposed, by the geological-survey report, to be about 4 feet above the mean surface of Lake Erie; hence the junction would be 21.90 above Lake Erie, or 594.98 feet above M. T. The elevation of this point by the G. T. R. W. is 591.27, a discrepancy of 3.71 feet. From this, and from the ninth determination of elevation of Lake Michigan, it appears that there is an error of about 4 feet in the M. C. R. R. profile, in the difference of elevation in its termini. The length of this line is two hundred and eighty-four miles.

Establishing the elevation of the Chicago directrix gives us the means of checking another very long line of levels, extending from M. T. at New Orleans to Chicago, a distance of nine hundred and sixty miles. The details of the line are as follows:

From mean tide at New Orleans to Chicago, by N. O. J. & Gt. N. R. R., Miss. C. R. R., M. & T. R. R., M. & L. R. R., N. & N. W. R R., H. W. slope of Mississippi River fourteen miles, M. & O. R. R., and Ill. C. R. R.

ELEVATION OF MEMPHIS, TENN.

	Feet.	Various datum-planes.	Elevation in feet above mean surface of Atlantic Ocean.
Canton, Miss., by N. O. J. & Gt. N. R. R	240.00	Above M. T. New Orleans	
Grenada, Miss., by Miss. C. R. R	56.00	Below Canton	
Memphis, L. W. in Mississippi River	0.00	Above Grenada	
Memphis, (supposed to be depot,) by M. & T. R. R.	75.00	......do	
Memphis, depot			259.00
Memphis, L. W			184.00
Memphis City datum + 100 feet = H. W. previous to 1858, by city-engineer report.	41.00	Below M. & T. R. R. depot	218.00
Grand Junction, Tenn., by M. C. R. R	334.44	Above Canton	
Grand Junction	574.44	Above New Orleans, M. T.	574.44
Memphis, by M. & C. R. R	329.47	Below Grand Junction	
Memphis, depot M. & C. R. R			244.97
Memphis, H. W. of railroad reports, 1844	25.00	Below M. & C. depot	219.97
Memphis City datum + 100 feet = H. W. previous to 1858.	27.00	Below M. & C. depot	217.97
(This city datum + 100 feet = H. W. is either the H. W. of 1844 or of 1850; but they differed only 0.4 foot. The elevation of this H. W. mark in several reports of the M. & C. R. R. is given as 220.44 above tide in Mobile Bay. As the only records that I have of the M. & C. R. R. are above L. T., Mobile Bay, this 220.44 may be above L. T. In this case Memphis H. W. would be 218.74 above Mobile Bay M. T., but in either case the results from New Orleans and Mobile differ very little.)			
Final results.			
Memphis H. W. previous to 1858, 100 feet above city-datum.		Above New Orleans M. T.	218.00
Do		......do	219.97
Do		......do	217.97
Mean of the above adopted result.			
Memphis H. W. 100 feet above city-datum		Above New Orleans, M. T.	218.65
Memphis H. W. 100 feet above city-datum	220.44	Above Mobile Bay	
Do	218.74	Above Mobile Bay, M. T.	

MEMPHIS TO CHICAGO.

	Feet.	Various datum-planes.	Elevation in feet above mean surface of Atlantic Ocean.
Memphis, Tenn., City datum + 100 feet = H. W. previous to 1858, by N. O. J. & G. N., M. C., M. & T. R. Rs.	218.65	Above M. T. New Orleans.	
McKenzie Junction, by M. & L. R. R	269.56	Above city-datum of Memphis + 100 feet = H. W.	
L. W. Mississippi River, Sept. 30, 1858, at Hickman, Ky.	213.00	Below McKenzie	
H. W., 1858, at Columbus, by Humphreys and Abbot's report.	37.80	Above L. W. 1858	
(This makes the H. W. slope of the river, from Hickman to Memphis, 0.49 feet per mile, supposing the distance to be 190 miles.)			
H. W. 1858, at Columbus, Ky., 14 miles up the Mississippi by slope of river.	7.00	Above H. W. Hickman	
H. W. at Cairo, by preliminary survey for M. & O. R. R.	11.50	Above H. W. at Columbus.	
Chicago directrix, by chief engineer I. C. R. R., October, 1873.	258.50	Above H. W. at Cairo	

MEMPHIS TO CHICAGO—Continued.

	Feet.	Various datum-planes.	Elevation in feet above mean surface of Atlantic Ocean.
Chicago directrix	....	Above M. T. New Orleans.	590. 01
From the figures given above we have also Memphis, Tenn., H. W. = city datum + 100 feet.	....	Above New Orleans M. T.	218. 65
Memphis, H. W. 1858	1. 00	Above previous extreme H. W.	....
Do	....	Above New Orleans M. T.	219. 65
Hickman, Ky., H. W. 1858	....	....	313. 01
Columbus, Ky., H. W. 1858	....	....	320. 01
Cairo, H. W. 1858	....	....	331. 51
Cairo City datum=ordinary L. W	40. 38	Below H. W. 1858	291. 13

The adopted elevation of the Chicago directrix being 587.15, this line of levels, nine hundred and sixty miles long, reaches Chicago with an error of only 2.86 feet. The error of connection, due to using the H. W. slope of the Mississippi River for fourteen miles, would not probably exceed a foot or two. At Memphis, the line is checked to within 1.8 feet with the levels from Mobile Bay. At Columbus and at Cairo, the line is checked by the M. & O. R. R.; but the only reports of this line which I can find give the elevations as determined by an experimental survey, the results of which were reported to the second meeting of stockholders, in 1850. The character of reconnaissance-surveys is such, and the results have proved so inaccurate when I have been able to compare them with the construction-levels, that I have not felt justified in giving the results of the M. & O. R. R. preliminary survey to Columbus and Cairo any weight as compared with the profiles of constructed lines. It is, however, upon this preliminary survey that Humphreys and Abbot, in their Hydraulics of the Mississippi River, base their elevations of Saint Louis, Cairo and Columbus, and consequently their slope of the river from Cairo to Memphis.

RESULTS BY M. & O. R. R., PRELIMINARY, COMPARED WITH ADOPTED LEVELS.

	Feet.	Various datum-planes.	Elevation in feet above mean surface of Atlantic Ocean.
H. W. at Columbus, by M. & O. preliminary survey	308. 50	Above M. L. W. Mobile Bay	....
M. T. Mobile Bay	1. 70	Above M. L. T	....
H. W. Columbus, by M. & O. preliminary	306. 80	Above M. T. Mobile Bay	306. 80
H. W. 1858, Columbus, by N. O. J. & G. N., M. C., M. & T., M. & L., N. & N. W. R. R.	320. 01	Above M. T. New Orleans.	320. 01
H. W. Cairo, by M. & O. preliminary	320.	Above L. T. Mobile Bay	....
Do	....	Above M. T. Mobile Bay	318. 30
H. W. 1858, Cairo, by N. O. J. & G. N., M. C., M. & T., M. & L., N. & N. W. R. R.	....	....	331. 51

It will be seen further on that the elevation of the Cairo City datum, as brought from New Orleans, is within a foot of that brought from the Cleveland directrix, via Cincinnati and Indianapolis. In summing up all evidence on the elevation of the Cairo City datum, on page 647, it will be shown why I reject the levels of the M. & O. R. R.

If we consider now the line from Portland to Chicago and from Chicago to New Orleans as one, we have a connected chain of railroad-levels twenty-one hundred miles long, starting from mean tide at Portland, Me., and reaching New Orleans, La., with an error of −9.9 feet.

If we join the N. Y. C. and L. S. & M. S. R. Rs. with the line from Chicago to New Orleans, we have a connected chain of railroad-levels, eighteen hundred miles long, starting from mean tide in New York Bay and ending at mean tide New Orleans, with an error of only −2.44 feet.

Using the Pa. R. R. and P. F. W. & C. R. R. for a through-connection in the same way between mean tide Raritan Bay and New Orleans mean tide, a distance of about eighteen hundred miles, the levels reach New Orleans with an error of −4.61 feet.

These results will give some idea of the accuracy of extended lines of railroad-levels when properly connected.

ELEVATION OF CINCINNATI CITY BASE, WHICH IS STANDARD LOW WATER IN OHIO RIVER, 62.50FEET BELOW H. W. 1832.

•	Feet.	Various datum-planes.	Elevation in feet above mean surface of Atlantic Ocean.
First determination.			
L. W. Ohio River at Cincinnati, by Miami and Erie Canal.	133.00	Below Lake Erie	
Mean surface of Lake Erie			573.08
L. W. at Cincinnati			440.08
Second determination.			
Columbus, Ohio, by C. C. C. & I. R. R	167.33	Above Cleveland directrix	
Cleveland directrix			575.68
Columbus, Ohio			743.01
L. W. in Ohio River at Cincinnati water-works, by Col. & X. and L. M. R. R.	307.58	Below Columbus depot	
L. W. Cincinnati			435.43
Third determination.			
Columbus, Ohio, depot track, by C. C. C. & I. from Cleveland directrix.			743.01
Athens, Ohio, junction of M. & C., by C. & H. V. R. R	96.00	Below Columbus depot	
Athens at junction of M. & C			647.01
L. W. at Cincinnati point, 62.5 feet below H. W. 1832, = city base, by M. & C. R. R.	207.00	Below Athens	
City base L. W. Cincinnati			440.01
Fourth determination.			
Dayton, by D. & M. R. R	180.00	Above Lake Erie at Toledo.	
L. W. at Cincinnati, by C. H. & D. R. R	313.00	Below Dayton	
Mean surface of Lake Erie			573.08
L. W. Cincinnati			440.08
Fifth determination.			
L. W. Ohio River at Parkersburgh, by report of a line of levels run from Cincinnati to Parkersburgh, (not the M. & C. R. R.)		Above M. T. Baltimore	573.50
L. W. in Ohio at Cincinnati, by same report		do	440.00
Final results.			
L. W. in Ohio River at Cincinnati, city directrix:			
(10) First determination			440.08
(1) Second determination			435.43
(1) Third determination			440.01
(1) Fourth determination			440.08
(1) Fifth determination			440.00
Mean with weights			439.74
Adopted result			439.74
(The first determination is given a weight of (10) because it is a canal-line. The second and third determinations are well checked at Columbus by the P. C. & St. L. R. R. from Pittsburgh.)			
Adopted elevation of Pittsburgh			746.00
Columbus depot track, by P. C. & St. L. R. R	3.80	Below Pittsburgh	
Columbus depot track			742.20

This result differs but 0.8 feet from that by the C. C. C. & I. R. R. from Cleveland directrix.

If we consider the depot track at Columbus, Ohio, as the point of junction of two long, connected lines of levels from the sea, one being from New York by the Erie Canal, surface of Lake Erie, C. C. C. & I. R. R., and the other by the Pa. R. R. and the P. C. & St. L. R. R., we should have the elevation of Columbus by the former as 743.01 feet above the sea, and by the latter as 741.11 feet. The difference between the two is only 1.9 feet, though the shorter line of the two is over six hundred miles in length.

ELEVATION OF INDIANAPOLIS.

	Feet.	Various datum-planes.	Elevation in feet above mean surface of Atlantic Ocean.
Cincinnati L. W., city-base			439.74
First determination.			
Cambridge, by W. W. Val. R. R	508.00	Above city-base	
Cambridge			947.74
Indianapolis union depot, by P. C. & St. L. R. R	227.00	Below Cambridge	
Indianapolis union depot			720.74
Second determination.			
Indianapolis union depot, by I. C. & L. R. R	283.01	Above point supposed to be city-base because H. W. 1858 is 58 feet in profile.	
Indianapolis union depot track			722.75
Third determination.			
City-datum of Fort Wayne, by report of city-engineer, who says it was brought by canal. As this elevation of the city-datum is not from original canal-reports, I do not dare to accept it, and prefer the following, as previous results have shown the C. C. C. & I. and P. F. W. & C. to be so reliable.	196.00	Above Lake Erie	769.08
Crestline, by C. C. C. & I. R. R	577.33	Above Cleveland directrix.	
Fort Wayne depot	348.00	Below Crestline	
Do	229.33	Above Cleveland directrix.	
Cleveland directrix			575.68
Fort Wayne depot of P. F. W. & C			805.01
City-datum, by city-engineer	15.31	Below P. F. W. & C. depot.	
Fort Wayne, city-datum			789.70
Fort Wayne, F. W. J. & S. R. R. depot	8.1	Below city-datum	
Junction of F. W. M. & C. R. R	6.0	Above F. W. J. & S. depot.	
Do			787.60
Cambridge, by F. W. M. & C. R. R	173.88	Above junction	
Cambridge			961.48
Indianapolis union depot, by P. C. & St. L	227.00	Below Cambridge	
Indianapolis union depot			734.48
(As it is not known that the depots at Fort Wayne, referred to by the railroad-profiles, are the same as those of the city-engineer's report, I do not feel certain of the connections by this line. I, therefore, reject this determination, and use only the first and second in the final result.)			
Final results.			
Indianapolis union depot:			
First determination	720.74		
Second determination	722.75		
Mean adopted			721.75
City-base Indianapolis is L. W. in White River	33.08	Below union depot	
Indianapolis city-base			688.67

ELEVATION OF THE SAINT LOUIS DIRECTRIX.

	Feet.	Various datum-planes.	Elevation in feet above mean surface of Atlantic Ocean.
First determination.			
Indianapolis union depot track			721.75
Terre Haute, by T. H. and Ind. R. R	217.00	Below union depot Indianapolis.	
Terre Haute, T. H. & Ind. depot			504.75
Terre Haute, H. W. in Wabash River	19.3	Below depot	
Do			485.45
Terre Haute, river-bed Wabash River	50.8	Below depot	
Do			453.95
Terre Haute, ordinary water Wabash River			467.45
Saint Louis directrix, by St. L. V. & T. H. R. R	71.60	Below Terre Haute depot.	
Saint Louis directrix			433.15
Second determination.			
Indianapolis union depot			721.75
Vincennes, by Ind. & V. R. R	287.36	Below Indianapolis union depot.	
Vincennes			434.39
Saint Louis directrix, by C. & V. and St. L. & S. E. R. Rs.	3.60	Below Vincennes	
Saint Louis directrix			430.79
Third determination.			
Cincinnati directrix			339.74
Present depot of O. & M. R. R., by city-engineer	54.94	Above city-directrix	
Vincennes, by O. & M. R. R. report in 1857	68.00	Below O. & M. Cincinnati depot.	
(It is not known whether the present depot is referred to in this old profile. If not the present one, it is probably the one at the north edge of the city, which is a few feet higher. Assuming it to be the same depot as at present:)			
Vincennes			326.68
(On account of the uncertainty above mentioned, this result is not used, but merely introduced to show how small the probable error is of the elevations of Indianapolis, and Vincennes as determined through Indianapolis.)			
Fourth determination.			
Chicago directrix			587.15
Effingham, by Ill. Cent. R. R., (Chicago branch,) reported to me by chief engineer, October, 1873.	10.50	Above Chicago directrix	
Saint Louis directrix, by St. L. V. & T. H. R. R	170.80	Below Effingham	
Saint Louis directrix			426.85
Fifth determination.			
Chicago directrix			587.15
Mendota, (Ill. C. R. R. crossing,) by C. B. & Q. R. R	169.07	Above Chicago directrix	
Vandalia, (exact crossing of St. L. V. & T. H. R. R.,) by Ill. C. R. R.	249.00	Below Mendota	
Saint Louis directrix, by St. L. V. & T. H. R. R	83.6	Below Vandalia	
Saint Louis directrix			423.62
Sixth determination.			
H. W. 1858, Columbus, Ky., by N. O. J. & Gt. N., M. C., M. & T., M. & L., N. & N. W. R. Rs. to Hickman, thence fourteen miles by river-slope.	320.01	Above M. T. New Orleans	
H. W. 1844, probably	319.11	do	
Saint Louis directrix, by St. L. & I. M. R. R	100.3	Above end of track at Belmont.	
(Belmont depot is certainly not below H. W. at Columbus, on the opposite side of the Mississippi River:)			
Hence by this route the Saint Louis directrix could not be less than.			419.41
Seventh determination.			
Memphis, H. W., city-base + 100 feet	218.65	Above M. T. New Orleans	
Argenta, (opposite Little Rock,) by M. & L. R. R. R	86.00	Above city-datum + 100 feet.	

ELEVATION OF THE SAINT LOUIS DIRECTRIX--Continued.

	Feet.	Various datum-planes.	Elevation in feet above mean surface of Atlantic Ocean.
Argenta			304.65
Saint Louis directrix, by C. & F. and St. L. & Q. M. R. Rs.	119.00	Above Little Rock	
(Assuming that the tracks are same height on both sides of the river at Little Rock:)			
Saint Louis directrix			423.65
Eighth determination.			
Cairo city-datum, ordinary L. W	291.13	Above New Orleans M. T.	
Carmi, by C. & V. R. R. and city-engineer	123.70	Above Cairo city-datum	
Saint Louis directrix, by St. L. & S. E. R. R	12.2	Above Carmi	
Saint Louis directrix		Above New Orleans M. T.	427.03
Ninth determination.			
Cairo H. W., by M. & O. R. R., preliminary line	318.30	Above M. T. Mobile Bay	
Saint Louis directrix, by C. & V. and St. L. & S. E. R. Rs	93.4	Above H. W. Cairo	
Saint Louis directrix			411.70
Saint Louis directrix, by Ill. Cent. to Vandalia, thence by St. L. & T. H. R. Rs.	96.6	Above Cairo H. W	
Saint Louis directrix			414.90
Final results.			
Saint Louis directrix:			
(1) First determination	433.15		
(1) Second determination	430.79		
Third determination			
(1) Fourth determination	426.85		
(1) Fifth determination	423.62		
(0) Sixth determination	[419.41]	Above New Orleans M. T.	
(0) Seventh determination	[423.65]	do	
(1) Eighth determination	427.03	do	
(0) Ninth determination	[411.70] [414.90]	Above Mobile M. T.	
Mean of five	428.29		
Adopted results.			
Saint Louis directrix			428.29
Saint Louis H. W. 1844			435.87
Saint Louis H. W. 1858			431.57
Saint Louis H. W. 1851			431.17
Saint Louis L. W., extreme			394.48

I have rejected the sixth determination because of the uncertainty of the connection at Belmont, and the seventh from the uncertainty of the connection at Little Rock. The two results of the ninth are rejected because they are the results of a mere preliminary survey on a line about five hundred miles long. The remainder are given equal weight because Cincinnati and Chicago are about equally distant from Saint Louis, and the connections equally good. The best result on the elevation of Saint Louis will be obtained when the C. A. & St. L. R. R. rerun their levels; their own engineer making the connection with the city-directrixes at both termini. If these levels are run with care, the elevation of Saint Louis, as deduced by them from the Chicago directrix, should, I think, supersede the one I have adopted. The elevation of the Saint Louis directrix, as given in Humphreys and Abbot's Report on the Hydraulics of the Mississippi River, is 405 feet. The causes of their error were the adoption of the elevation of Cairo H. W. above Mobile Bay, as determined by the preliminary line of the M. & O. R. R., and of the elevation of Saint Louis above Cairo, as reported by Gen. G. B. McClellan. His report was based on a connection of the I. C. R. R., and the O. & M. R. R. This part of the O. & M. R. R. profile cannot now be had.

His elevation of Saint Louis directrix above H. W. Cairo is 82.9 feet. By connecting the Ill. Cent. with the St. L. V. & T. H. R. R. at Vandalia, my result for the difference of elevation of these points is 96.6 feet; by Ill. Cent. R. R. to Decatur, and T. W. & W. R. R. to Saint Louis, 96 feet; by Ill. Cent. to Effingham and St. L. V. & T. H. R. R. to Saint Louis, 98.2 feet; by C. & V. and St. L. & S. E. R. R.s, 93.4 feet; and by a preliminary survey for railroad from Saint Louis to Ca ro, 102 feet. The mean of my four determinations by constructed lines, the preliminary-survey result of 102 feet being excluded, is 96.05 feet for the elevation of Saint Louis directrix above H. W. at Cairo.

I hope the evidence that I have presented will be considered as warranting this important change of 23.3 feet that I have made in the elevation of Saint Louis and the fall of the Mississippi River.*

ELEVATION OF OMAHA.

	Feet.	Various datum planes.	Elevation in feet above mean surface of Atlantic Ocean.
First determination.			
Dubuque, Mississippi River, by a report from Mr. J. A. Lapham, Milwaukee.	10.00	Above Lake Michigan	
Dubuque, L. W. Mississippi River, by Galena & Chi. R. R.	13.00	do	
Dubuque, adopted L. W	12.00	do	
Lake Michigan, mean surface			589.15
Dubuque, L. W. Mississippi River			601.15
Sioux City, track on levee, by Ill. Cent. R. R., Iowa division.	522.50	Above L. W. at Dubuque	
Sioux City, track on levee	534.20	Above Lake Michigan	
Do			1,123.35
Mo. Valley junction with C. & N. W. R. R., by S. C. & P. R. R.	90.6	Below S. C. track on levee.	
Mo. Valley junction			1,032.75
Council Bluffs station, by C. & N. W. R. R	20.00	Below M. V. junction	
Council Bluffs station			1,012.75
Missouri River	31.00	Below M. V. junction	
Do			1,001.75
Council Bluffs, Missouri River L. W., by two other reports of C. & N. W. R. R.	31.00	Below M. V. junction	
Council Bluffs, L. W. Missouri River			1,001.75
Check upon first determination.			
Frémont, by S. C. & P. R. R	190.3	Above M. V. junction	
Frémont			1,223.05
Omaha, L. W. mark base of U. P., by U. P. R. R	236.00	Below Frémont	
Do			987.05

This latter result is evidently the correct one; for if L. W. was only 11 feet below the Council Bluffs station, as is reported by the C. & N. W. R. R., then their station would be overflowed 8 feet in time of high water. By the careful leveling of the bridge-company at Omaha, the flat alluvial regions on both sides of the Missouri River were shown to be about twenty feet above L. W. Hence, I reject the report of low water by the C. & N. W. R. R., and by levels from Council Bluffs station across to the U. P. R. R. L. W. base at Omaha. The various old and new datums on the Council Bluffs side of the river cannot differ over 2 feet in height.

* Since the above was written, I have found a report of the Saint Louis and Iron Mt. R. R. surveys, signed by J. H. Morley, chief engineer, giving H. W. in Mississippi River, at Ohio City, opposite Cairo, as 97 feet below the Saint Louis directrix, and H. W., Mississippi River, New Madrid, as 126 feet below Saint Louis directrix.

	Feet.	Various datum-planes.	Elevation in feet above mean surface of Atlantic Ocean.
Omaha, L. W. base of U. P. R. R. surveys, by leveling of bridge-engineers.	21.80	Below Council Bluffs station.	....
Council Bluffs station			1,012.72
Omaha, L. W. base of U. P. R. R			990.95
Second determination.			
Council Bluffs station, by C. & N. W. R. R	420.9	Above Lake Michigan	....
Lake Michigan mean surface			589.15
Council Bluffs station			1,010.05
Omaha, L. W. base of U. P. R. R	21.80	Below Council Bluffs	....
Do			988.25
Third determination.			
Rock Island depot track, by C. R. I. & P. R. R	(8) 20.00	Below Lake Michigan	....
Rock Island depot track, by C. B. & Q. to Monmouth, thence by R. R. I. & St. L. R. R.	(1) 20.03	Below Chicago directrix	....
Rock Island depot track, by C. R. I. & P. to Peoria, and P. & R. I. R. R.	(1) 22.70	Below Lake Michigan	....
(Assuming the above as referring to mean surface of Lake Michigan, I adopt the mean with weights as marked, giving much the greater weight to the direct through-line.)			
Adopted result for Rock Island depot track	20.47	Below mean, Lake Michigan.	....
Do	18.47	Below Chicago directrix	....
Do			568.68
Davenport depot track, corner of Fifth and Perry streets, by line of levels run for United States Weather-Bureau, 1872.	23.20	Above Rock Island depot track.	....
Davenport, old depot track			591.88
Davenport, L. W. datum of C. R. I. & P. and P. & S. W. R. R.	32.00	Below depot at Davenport	....
Davenport, C. R. I. & P. R. R datum			559.88
Council Bluffs station-grounds	432.00	Above Davenport datum	....
Do			991.88
Omaha, L. W. base of U. P. R. R	21.80	Below Council Bluffs station.	....
Do			970.08
Fourth determination.			
Burlington, L. W. datum of B. & M. R. R., by C. B. & Q. R. R.	75.26	Below Chicago directrix	....
Burlington L. W., B. & M. R. R. datum			511.89
East Plattsmouth, H. W. Missouri River	438.30	Above datum at Burlington	....
East Plattsmouth, L. W. Missouri River	421.30	......do	....
East Plattsmouth, H. W. Missouri River			950.19
East Plattsmouth, L. W. Missouri River, by B. & M. R. R.			933.19
Kearney junction, by B. & M. and P. R. Rs	1,629.00	Above L. W. datum at Burlington.	....
Do			2,140.89
Omaha, L. W. base of U. P. R. R., by U. P. R. R	1,179.00	Below Kearney junction	....
Omaha, L. W. base of U. P. R. R			961.89
Fifth determination.			
Moberly, by St. L. K. C. & N. R. R	454.37	Above Saint Louis directrix.	....
Saint Louis directrix			428.29
Hannibal H. W. 1851	397.50	Below Moberly	....
Do	56.87	Above Saint Louis directrix.	....
Do			485.16
Quincy, L. W. 1854, by C. B. & Q. R. R	114.76	Below Chicago directrix	....
Quincy, H. W. 1851	94.04	......do	....
Hannibal, H. W. 1851, by slope of river at one-half foot per mile.	8.00	Below Quincy H. W	....
Hannibal, H. W. 1851	102.04	Below Chicago directrix	....
Do			485.11
Saint Joseph, H. W. Missouri River, by H. & St. J. R. R.	335.00	Above H. W. Hannibal	....
Do			820.11

	Feet.	Various datum-planes.	Elevation in feet above mean surface of Atlantic Ocean.
Kearney junction, by St. J. & D. R. R.	1,343.00	Above H. W. at Saint Joe	
Kearney junction			2,163.11
Omaha, L. W. base of U. P. R. R.	1,179.00	Below Kearney junction	
Do			984.11
Final results.			
L. W. base of U. P. R. R. at Omaha:			
(2) First determination	987.05	By S. C. & P., by Fremont.	
(3) Second determination	988.25	By C. & N. W. R. R.	
(3) Third determination	970.08	By C. R. I. & P. R. R.	
(2) Fourth determination	961.89	By B. & M. and U. P. from Kearney Junction.	
(1) Fifth determination	984.11	By Saint Joe and U. P. from Kearney Junction.	
Mean with weights	977.90		
Adopted result.			
L. W. base of U. P. R. R. at Omaha			977.90
(The old 966-foot point given as Omaha on the published profiles of the U. P. R. R., was a stone standing upon the bank of the river. It is now washed away.)			
Stone on river-bank called 966 feet above sea	20.00	Above L. W. base	
Do			997.90
Present depot-grounds on main line U. P. R. R.	82.50	Above L. W. base	1,060.40

From this determination of Omaha, it seems that 31.9 feet must be added to all the elevations of the U. P. R. R. to give the true height above the sea; but the range among the results is so large that the leveling across Iowa must be very poor as compared with that of the lines east of the Mississippi River.

Omaha cannot be considered as well determined as Kansas City; but this mean of five level-lines is much more probable than the old determination, which rested on barometric observations.

ELEVATION OF KANSAS CITY.

	Feet.	Various datum-planes.	Elevation in feet above mean surface of Atlantic Ocean.
First determination.			
Kansas City, H. W. 1844, mark on abutment of railroad-bridge, by Mo. P. R. R., reported to me by general superintendent, Mr. Talmadge, October, 1873.	342.00	Above Saint Louis directrix.	
Saint Louis directrix			428.29
Kansas City, H. W. mark 1844			770.29
Second determination.			
Junction of St. L. K. C. & N. R. R. and H. & St. J., by St. L. K. C. & N. R. R.	325.88	Above Saint Louis directrix.	
Kansas City, H. W. mark 1844, by line of levels run for us by city-engineer.	18.54	Above junction	
Kansas City, H. W. mark 1844	344.42	Above Saint Louis directrix.	
Do			772.71

	Feet.	Various datum-planes.	Elevation in feet above mean surface of Atlantic Ocean.
Third determination.			
Quincy, H. W. 1851, by C. B. & Q. R. R	94.04	Below Chicago directrix	
Quincy, H. W. 1851			493.11
Hannibal, H. W. by slope of river one-half foot per mile.	8.00	Below Quincy H. W	
Hannibal, H. W. 1851			485.11
Kansas City, by H. & St. J. R. R	375.00	Above Hannibal H. W. 1851.	
Kansas City			760.11
Kansas City, H. W. 1844	11.25	Above old St. J. R. R. depot	
Do			771.36
Fourth determination.			
Davenport, C. R. I. & P. R. R. datum			559.88
Leavenworth railroad-bridge, by C. R. I. & P. R. R., southwest division.	271.00	Above Davenport datum	
Leavenworth railroad-bridge track			830.88
Bridge over Five-Mile Creek, Leavenworth, by special levels run by city-engineer.	56.21	Below track of railroad-bridge.	
Bridge over Five-Mile Creek, track of L. & L. R. R.			774.67
Junction of the L. & L. branch with K. P. R. R., main line.	49.00	Above Five-Mile Creek	
Junction L. & L. and K. P. R. Rs			823.67
Kansas City track at State line	68.00	Below L. & L. junction	
Do			755.67
Kansas City, H. W. 1844	7.25	Above K. P. track at State line.	
Do			762.92
Final results.			
Kansas City, H. W. 1844, marked on abutment of railroad-bridge:			
(5) First determination	770.29	By Mo. P. R. R	
(5) Second determination	772.71	By St. L. K. C. & N. R. R	
(1) Third determination	771.36	By H. & St. J. R. R	
(1) Fourth determination	762.92	By C. R. I. & P., southwestern division.	
Mean with weights	770.77		
Adopted result.			
Kansas City, H. W. 1844			770 77

I have given the greater weights to the first and second determinations, which come directly from Saint Louis directrix, each one being a continuous line, run under the direction of one company. The old elevation for Kansas City H. W. 1844 was 655.51. This determination was reported by Mr. O. Chanute, chief engineer K. C. bridge, to Mr. E. C. Smead, chief engineer of the K. P. R. R., July 14, 1870, and has been used not only by the K. P. R. R. but by all the other lines diverging from Kansas City. The altitudes above sea given by all these lines need therefore to be increased about 115 feet. The cause of Mr. Chanute's main error was due to a false report of the profile of the Mo. P. R. R. height of H. W. 1844, K. C. above the Saint Louis directrix. He gives this height as 252.51 feet, when it should have been 352.51, which was the old result from computing their levels. I have four reports from this railroad, including Mr. Chanute's. The report given me personally by Mr. Talmadge, chief engineer and general superintendent, in October, 1873, gives 342 feet; another report, by the same gentleman, 351 feet; a report by Mr. E. Miller, 342.35 feet; and Mr. Chanute's report, 252.51 feet. I think the evidence conclusive that the report of 252.51 feet, heretofore relied on for this difference of elevation, was intended for 352.51, but altered in copying. The remainder of the error was due to assuming the old elevation of the Saint Louis directrix.

ELEVATION OF DENVER, COLO.

	Feet.	Various datum-planes.	Elevation in feet above mean surface of Atlantic Ocean.
First determination.			
State-line, eastern terminus of K. P. R. R. track	7.25	Below H. W. 1844, Kansas City.	
Kansas City, H. W. 1844			770.77
State-line, K. P. R. R. track			763.52
Denver junction of K. P. & D. P. R. R., by K. P. R. R.	4,448.70	Above State-line	
Denver junction			5,212.22
Denver, D. P. & K. P. R. R. depot track, by D. P. profile.	13.25	Below junction	
Denver, D. P. & K. P. passenger-depot track			5,198.97
Second determination.			
Cheyenne, U. P. depot track, by U. P. R. R.	5,095.00	Above Omaha U. P. R. R., L. W. datum.	
Omaha, U. P. L. W. datum			977.90
Cheyenne, U. P. R. R. depot track			6,072.90
Denver, D. P. & K. P. R. R. depot, by D. P. R. R.	878.70	Below Cheyenne	
Denver, K. P. & D. P. R. R. passenger-depot track			5,194.20
Third determination.			
Construction-station 3985, near Pine Bluff, on U. P. R. R., by U. P. R. R.	4,113.00	Above Omaha L. W. datum	
Station 3985			5,090.90
Denver, D. P. depot, by a D. P. R. R. preliminary	101.45	Above station 3985 U. P. R. R.	
Denver, D. P. depot			5,192.35
Final results.			
(1) First determination	5,198.97	By K. P. R. R	
(1) Second determination	5,194.20	By U. P. R. R. & D. P	
(0) Third determination	5,192.35	By D. P. preliminary	
Mean with weights	5,196.58		
Adopted result.			
Denver, D. P. & K. P. R. R. passenger-depot track			5,196.58
Difference from the mean, by K. P. R. R	+ 2.39		
Difference by U. P. R. R	− 2.38		

The third determination is given no weight as against the construction-levels of the same railroad. Such a close agreement between the U. P. and K. P. lines was not to be expected when we realize that for the last thousand miles they are really independent, one being from Chicago, by way of Saint Louis and Kansas City, and the other by way of Omaha and Cheyenne. Though Denver is two thousand miles from the sea, this determination of its elevation is probably very close to the result that would be obtained by the most accurate line of levels run across the country for scientific purposes; but a considerable error must pertain to all results from the effect of the mass of the Rocky Mountains in deflecting the level from a truly horizontal position. We cannot tell how much this error is until a most accurate geodetic belt is completed from the Atlantic to the Rocky Mountains, and then, knowing the station-errors or the deflection of the plumb-line along the belt, we may correct the leveling proportionally. As this cannot be done for many years, the elevation of Denver, as here determined, will be made the base for our hypsometric surveys in the Rocky Mountains.

ELEVATION OF CHEYENNE.

	Feet.	Various datum-planes.	Elevation in feet above mean surface of Atlantic Ocean.
Cheyenne, U. P. passenger-depot track, by D. P. R. R.	878. 70	Above Denver	
Denver			5, 196. 58
Cheyenne, U. P. passenger-depot track			6, 075. 28

ELEVATION OF GOLDEN DIRECTRIX.

Golden directrix, by C. C. R. R.	519. 9	Above south Y junction near Denver.	
South Y at junction, by D. P. R. R	12. 5	Above Denver depot	
Golden directrix	532. 4	do	
Do			5, 728. 98

ELEVATION OF OGDEN, UTAH.

Cheyenne			6, 075. 28
Ogden depot, by U. P. R. R	1, 749. 00	Below Cheyenne	
Ogden			4, 326. 28
Second determination.			
Ogden depot, by C. P. R. R.	4, 301	Above Pacific Ocean	
Ogden			4, 301. 00
Final result.			
(1) First determination	4, 326. 28	By U. P. R. R	
(10) Second determination	4, 301. 00	By C. P. R. R.	
Mean with weights	4, 303. 3		
Adopted result.			
Ogden depot track			4, 303. 3

The result by the Central Pacific of California is given much the greater weight, because it is a continuous line of levels run by one railroad company, the same chief engineer, Mr. S. S. Montague, superintending the running of all the lines and the making-up of preliminary and final profiles. The length, also, of this line is only about one-third of that from the Atlantic Ocean.

If we consider these lines as one long chain of levels from the Atlantic to the Pacific, we have connected railroad-levels extending not less than thirty-five hundred miles, and reaching the Pacific Ocean with an error of 25 feet. If we form a continuous line of levels by joining those of the Pa., P. F. W. & C., C. R. I. & P., U. P., and C. P. R. R.s, they reach the Pacific with an error of +13 feet.

If a chain is formed by putting together the lines from New Orleans to Cairo; thence by I. M. R. R. to Saint Louis; thence by Mo. P., K. P., D. P., U. P., and C. P. R. R.s, the line is thirty-two hundred miles long, and reaches the Pacific Ocean with an error of +26 feet. In this chain, the levels of eleven different railroads are connected.

ELEVATION OF COLORADO SPRINGS.

	Feet.	Various datum-planes.	Elevation in feet above mean surface of Atlantic Ocean.
(Denver depot of D. & R. G. R. W. track is reported to be one foot above D. P. R. R. track. This may be in error 0.2 foot. The following figures are taken from the official profile in use at the D. & R. G. R. R. company's office.)			
Denver, K. P. depot	5, 142. 6		
Denver depot D. & R. G. R. R	5, 143. 6		
Colorado Springs depot	5. 931. 6		
Colorado Springs	789. 0	Above Denver K. P. depot.	
Denver, D. P. & K. P. depot			5, 196. 58
Colorado Springs depot			5, 985. 58
Colorado Springs Hotel floor, by report of Mr. E. S. Nettleton, C. E.	826. 67	Above Denver K. P. depot.	
Colorado Springs Hotel floor			6, 023. 25
Rock basin of Manitou Spring, by levels from railroad-bench, by E. S. Nettleton, C. E.	1, 153. 32	Above Denver K. P. depot.	
Rock basin of Manitou Spring			6, 296. 92

Elevation of Pike's Peak.

I am greatly indebted to Mr. E. S. Nettleton, civil engineer, for a report dated June 29, 1874, of a line of levels which he has just run from a D. & R. G. R. W. bench at Colorado Springs to the exact summit of Pike's Peak. The line was run on the request of Gen. Albert J. Meyer, Chief Signal-Officer, U. S. A., and at the expense of the War Department, for determining the elevation of the United States Signal-Office meteorological station, which is situated on the summit of the peak.

	Feet.	Various datum-planes.	Elevation in feet above mean surface of Atlantic Ocean.
Exact highest rock on Pike's Peak	8, 950. 1	Above Denver K. P. depot.	
Do			14, 146. 68

Elevation of Mount Lincoln and Fairplay.

The D. & S. P. R. R. having run a line of levels for the final location of their railroad up to Fairplay, we secured the services of their engineer to continue the line to the summit of Mount Lincoln, at the expense of our survey. The object of this was to determine the exact elevation of our barometric station situated near the top of the peak. The following are the results of this line of railroad levels:

	Feet.	Various datum-planes.	Elevation in feet above mean surface of Atlantic Ocean.
Denver (D. P. & K. P.) depot			5,196.58
Door-sill of Sentinel office Fairplay	4,767.91	Above Denver depot	
Do			9,964.49
Cistern of Mount Lincoln barometer	8,991.05	Above Denver depot	
Do			14,187.63
Summit of Mount Lincoln	9,100.08	Above Denver depot	
Do			14,296.66

ELEVATION OF POINTS ON THE OHIO RIVER.

	Feet.	Various datum-planes.	Elevation in feet above mean surface of Atlantic Ocean.
Pittsburgh, union depot track			746.00
Pittsburgh, L. W. city-datum	46.80	Below Union depot track	
Do			699.20
Pittsburgh, H. W. 1852			729.88
Pittsburgh, H. W. 1832			732.95
(These data are from report of city engineer, March 15, 1871.)			
Steubenville P. C. & St. L. R. R. depot track, by P. C. & St. L. R. R.	14.74	Below Pittsburgh depot	
Steubenville depot, P. C. & St. L. R. R			731.26
Steubenville, L. W. in Ohio, by old P. & S. R. R	68.43	Below L. W. in Ohio at Pittsburgh.	
Steubenville, L. W. in Ohio			630.77
Steubenville, about H. W. 1852, by C. & P. R. R	103.55	Above Cleveland directrix	
Do			679.23
Bridgeport, about H. W. 1852, by C. & P. R. R	96.55	Above Cleveland directrix	
Bridgeport, about H. W. 1852			672.23
(Bridgeport is opposite Wheeling.)			
Bellaire, 5 miles below Bridgeport, about H. W. 1852, by C. & P. R. R.	84.55	Above Cleveland directrix	
Do			660.00
Wheeling, H. W. February 1832, by B. & O. R. R.			[637.00]
By the same report the channel is given at			[588.00]
(These B. & O. R. R. results are considered too low, as they give an improbable fall to the Ohio from Steubenville. The L. W. fall from Pittsburgh to Steubenville is known by the P. & S. R. R. survey to be about one foot per mile. The report of the C. & P. R. R. for Bellaire seems to give the most probable result. From Steubenville to Bellaire the distance by river is about twenty-eight miles, therefore L. W. at Bellaire, giving the maximum probable fall one foot per mile.)			
Bellaire, L. W. about	60.3	Above sea	
Bellaire, H. W. about	65.1	......do	
Bellaire, about H. W. 1852, by report of C. & P. R. R	84.55	Above Cleveland directrix	
Bellaire, about H. W. 1852			660.00
(This result is about what it should be, for it is not probable that the fall here is one foot per mile. If the B. & O. R. R. result was true, it would give the river a fall of 42 feet in 23 miles. I therefore consider it most probable that Wheeling H. W. 1852 is about 663 feet, and the B. & O. R. R. report of 637 for H. W. 1832 is some thirty feet too low.)			
Parkersburgh, by several reports of B. & O. R. R., point not given.	523.7	Above M. T., Baltimore	
By the report of the engineers running the line from Parkersburgh to Cincinnati, the B. & O. Parkersburgh L. W.	573.00	......do	
(I accept the latter, because it accords best with the next check at Point Pleasant, about seventy miles down the river.)			
Parkersburgh, L. W. in Ohio			573.00
Point Pleasant, very L. W. at mouth of Great Kanawha.	522.00	Above M. T., Richmond, Va.	
By two lines of levels agreeing within a foot			522.00
Portsmouth, Ohio, L. W. in Ohio River, by C. & X. R. R. report.	94.00	Below L. Erie	
Portsmouth, L. W			479.00
Cincinnati, L. W. city base			439.74
Indianapolis, union depot track	721.75	Above M. T	
Greencastle junction, by T. H. & I. R. R	56.00	Above Union depot, Indianapolis.	
New Albany, passenger depot	326.00	Below Greencastle	

	Feet.	Various datum-planes.	Elevation in feet above mean surface of Atlantic Ocean.
New Albany, L. W. in Ohio River, by L. N. A. & C. R. R.	398.00	Below Greencastle	
New Albany, passenger depot			451.75
New Albany, L. W. of 1857 in Ohio River			379.75
(This was not one of the years of lowest water, but it was probably about four feet above it.)			
Louisville, L. W	24.00	Above New Albany, L. W.	
Louisville, L. W. 1857			403.75
Evansville, L. W	81.00	Below Vincennes	
Evansville rail, by E. & C. V. R. R	36.00	do	
Vincennes	434.39	Above M. T.	
Evansville, L. W. Ohio River			353.39
Evansville, depot rail			398.39
Evansville, H. W. 1847	334.54	Below Union depot track	
By survey for E. & I. R. R., H. W. 1847			387.22
Evansville Railroad track, by St. L. & S. E. R. R	35.2	Below Saint Louis directrix	
Evansville Railroad track			393.08
Evansville, L. W			348.08

ELEVATION OF CAIRO.

	Feet.	Various datum-planes.	Elevation in feet above mean surface of Atlantic Ocean.
First determination.			
Cairo, I. C. R. R. track on levee, by C. & V. R. R	96.5	Below Vincennes	
Do			337.89
Cairo, H. W. Ohio River, by C. & V. R. R	97.00	Below Vincennes	
Do			337.39
Cairo city-base, by engineer in charge of levees	43.00	Below Illinois Central track	
Cairo city-base, ordinary L. W			294.89
Second determination.			
Cairo, H. W. Ohio River, by mean of four routes, (see discussion of change in Saint Louis directrix, p. —)	96.05	Below Saint Louis directrix	
Cairo, H. W. Ohio River			332.24
Cairo city-base	41.00	Below mean of highest floods	
Do			291.24
Third Determination.			
Cairo, H. W. 1858 in Ohio River		Above M. T. New Orleans	331.51
Cairo city-base			291.13
Fourth determination.			
Cairo, H. W. Ohio River	258.50	Below Chicago directrix	
Do			328.65
Cairo, city-base			287.65
Final results.			
Cairo city base:			
First determination	294.89	By Cincinnati	
Second determination	291.24	By Saint Louis	
Third determination	291.13	By New Orleans	
Fourth determination	287.65	By Chicago	
Mean	291.23		
Adopted result			291.23
(By report of engineer in charge of levee construction.)			
Cairo, extreme L. W. October 15, 1871	11.91	Below city-base	
Cairo, ordinary L. W	0.00		
Cairo, H. W. 1858	40.38	Above city-base	
Cairo, H. W. 1862	41.69	do	
Cairo, H. W. 1867	41.81	do	
Cairo, Illinois Central track on levee	43 to 43.5	do	
Cairo Hotel, northeast corner	43.26	do	
Cairo, Mississippi levee	44.00	do	

Elevations of points determined in this investigation.

NOTE.—The evidence upon which each rests may be seen by reference to the map and foregoing text.

Names of determined points.	State.	Elevation in feet above mean surface of Atlantic Ocean.
Albany, mean tide in Hudson River	New York	4.84
Altoona, track P. R. R. station	Pennsylvania	1,177.91
Alliance, track P. F. W. & C. R. R. station	Ohio	1,082.88
Atchison, H. W. Missouri River, (supposed to be 1844)	Kansas	809.88
Atchison, L. W. Missouri River	...do	784.88
Athens, railroad-station	Ohio	647.01
Belmont, track of St. L. & I. M. R. R	Missouri	328.00
Buffalo, bottom of Erie Canal	New York	564.26
Buffalo, theoretical surface of Erie Canal	...do	573.26
Buffalo mean surface of Lake Erie	...do	573.08
Burlington, H. W. 1851 in Mississippi River	Iowa	529.32
Burlington, L. W. Mississippi River	...do	511.89
Burlington, Main street depot	...do	531.61
Carmi, junction of C. & V. and St. L. & S. W. R. R	Illinois	416.09
Cambridge, W. W. Val. R. R. depot	Ohio	947.74
Cairo, city-base = ordinary L. W. Ohio River	Illinois	291.23
Cairo, extreme L. W. October 18, 1871, Ohio River	...do	279.32
Cairo, H. W. 1858, Ohio River	...do	331.61
Cairo, H. W. 1862, Ohio River	...do	332.92
Cairo, I. C. R. R. track on levee	...do	334.48
Canton depot	Mississippi	240.00
Cedar Rapids, C. & N. W depot	Iowa	741.15
Cedar Rapids, city-datum, L. W. foot of Iowa avenue	...do	717.85
Cheyenne, track at U. P. R. R. passenger-depot	Wyoming	6,075.28
Chicago, city directrix	Illinois	587.15
Chicago, mean surface of Lake Michigan for the past 20 years	...do	589.15
Cincinnati, city directrix = L. W. in Ohio River	Ohio	439.74
Cincinnati, H. W. 1832, Ohio River	...do	502.24
Cleveland, city directrix	Ohio	575.68
Cleveland, mean surface of Lake Erie	...do	573.08
Clinton, bridge over Mississippi River	Iowa	611.15
Clinton, H. W. 1864, Mississippi River	...do	593.15
Columbus, depot track of P. C. & St. L. and C. C. C. & I	Ohio	742.60
Columbus, H. W. 1858, Mississippi River	Kentucky	320.01
Colorado Springs, depot track D. & R. G. R. R	Colorado	5,985.58
Colorado Springs, Colorado Springs Hotel floor, (see Manitou)	...do	6,023.25
Council Bluffs, union depot track	Iowa	999.70
Crestline, P. F. W. & C. depot track	Ohio	1,152.74
Davenport, old depot track, corner Fifth and Perry streets	Iowa	591.88
Davenport, railroad level datum of C. R. I. & P	...do	559.88
Davenport, top of west abutment of railroad-bridge	...do	589.06
Davenport, H. W. Mississippi River	...do	569.88
Davenport, L. W. Mississippi River	...do	553.22
Davenport, city-base of levels	...do	547.88
Decatur, I. C. R. R. depot	Illinois	675.65
Denver, K. P. & D. P. R. R. depot track	Colorado	5,196.58
Denver, D. & R. G. R. R. depot track	...do	5,197.58
Detroit, mean surface of river	Michigan	577.05
Dubuque, L. W. Mississippi River, I. C. R. R. datum	Iowa	599.15
Effingham, I. C. R. R. depot track and St. L. V. & T. H. R. R. depot	Illinois	599.10
Erie, L. S. & M. S. R. R. depot track	Pennsylvania	686.68
Evansville, depot track	Indiana	395.60
Evansville, L. W. in Ohio River	...do	350.60
Evansville, H. W. 1847, Ohio River	...do	384.43
Fairplay, door-sill of Sentinel office before fire of 1873	Colorado	9,964.49
Fremont, U. P. R. R. depot track	Nebraska	1,213.90
Fulton, H. W. 1864, Mississippi River	Illinois	593,15
Gloucester Point, permanent United States Coast Survey bench on granite block	New Jersey	8.10
Gloucester, mean tide in Delaware River	...do	3.35
Golden, city and railroad directrix	Colorado	5,728.98
Grand Haven, mean surface of Lake Michigan	Michigan	589.15
Grenada depot	Mississippi	184.00
Greencastle, junction depot	Indiana	777.75
Hannibal, H. W. 1851, Mississippi River	Missouri	485.10
Harrisburgh, Pa. R. R. depot track	Pennsylvania	319.91
Hickman, H. W. 1858, Mississippi River	Kentucky	313.01
Indianapolis, Union depot track	Indiana	721.75
Indianapolis, city base L. W. in White River	...do	688.67
Kansas City, H. W. 1844 of Missouri River, as marked on abutment of R. R. Bridge	Missouri	770.77
Kansas City, track of K. P. R. W. at State line	...do	763.52
Kearney junction depot	Nebraska	2,156.90
Keokuk, C. B. & Q. R. R. depot	Iowa	508.22
Keokuk, city base	...do	487.72

Elevations of points determined in this investigation—Continued.

Names of determined points.	State.	Elevation in feet above mean surface of Atlantic Ocean.
Keokuk, H. W. 1851, Mississippi River	Iowa	502. 55
Keokuk, L. W. (extreme) Mississippi River	....do	481. 83
Lawrence, K. P. R. W. & L. & L. branch junction	Kansas	831. 52
Lawrence, K. P. R. W. depot track	....do	845. 52
Leavenworth, city-datum, extreme L. W. Missouri River, Jan., 1867	....do	763. 89
Leavenworth, H. W. Missouri River, (probably 1844)	....do	788. 89
Little Rock, C. & F. R. R. depot	Arkansas	309. 29
Louisville, L. W. in Ohio River, above falls*	Kentucky	403. 75
Lake Champlain, mean surface at Whitehall		100. 84
Lake Ontario, mean surface at Oswego		250. 00
Lake Erie, mean surface at Buffalo and Cleveland from 1844 to 1857		573. 08
Lake Michigan, mean surface since 1853 at Chicago		589. 15
Lake Huron		589. 15
Manitou Springs, rock around the Manitou Spring	Colorado	6, 296. 92
McKenzie junction depot	Tennessee	488. 21
Memphis, H. W. in Mississippi River previous to 1858, and is 100 feet above city-datum	....do	218. 65
Mendota, C. B. & Q. R. R. depot	Illinois	756. 22
Missouri Valley junction	Iowa	1, 019. 70
Mount Lincoln, extreme summit	....do	14, 296. 66
Mount Lincoln, cistern of barometer in 1873	....do	14, 187. 63
Montreal, summer water-level in river	Canada	30. 00
New Albany, depot of L. N. A. & C. R. R	Indiana	451. 75
New Albany, L. W. 1857, Ohio River	....do	379. 75
Ogden, U. P. & C. P. R. R. depot track	Utah	4, 303. 30
Omaha, base of levels of U. P. R. R., L. W. in Missouri River	Nebraska	977. 90
Omaha, H. W. in Missouri River	....do	996. 90
Omaha, bed of river	....do	964. 10
Omaha, bench heretofore called 966 feet above the sea	....do	997. 90
Omaha, track at present depot in main line U. P. R. R.	....do	1, 030. 40
Omaha, tops of east and west abutments of railroad-bridge	....do	1, 049. 40
Oswego, mean surface of Lake Ontario	New York	250. 00
Parkersburgh, L. W. in Ohio River	West Virginia	573. 00
Peoria, city-datum, L. W. in Illinois River	Illinois	439. 00
Peoria, C., R. I. & P. R. R. depot	....do	464. 70
Pittsburgh, Union depot track	Pennsylvania	746. 00
Pittsburgh, city-datum, L. W. in river	....do	699. 20
Pittsburgh, H. W. 1852	....do	729. 88
Pittsburgh, H. W. 1832	....do	732. 95
Pike's Peak, exact summit	Colorado	14, 146. 68
Pike's Peak, top of U. S. G. & G. survey monument on east side of summit	....do	14, 124. 84
Philadelphia, city-datum	Pennsylvania	8. 733
Philadelphia, Pa. R. R. datum or base of levels	....do	6. 913
Philadelphia, mean tide in Delaware River	....do	3. 349
Philadelphia, high tide in Delaware River	....do	6. 484
Philadelphia, low tide in Delaware River	....do	0. 214
Point Pleasant, very L. W. in Ohio River	West Virginia	522. 00
Portsmouth, L. W. in Ohio River	Ohio	479. 00
Port Huron, mean surface of Lake Huron	Michigan	589. 15
Port Sarnia, mean surface of Lake Huron	Canada West	589. 15
Port Sarnia, G. W. R. W. track	....do	593. 15
Prairie Du Chien, probable L. W. in Mississippi River	Wisconsin	613. 00
Quincy, C., B. & Q. R. R. depot	Illinois	495. 22
Quincy, L. W. 1854 Mississippi River	....do	472. 39
Quincy, H. W. 1851 Mississippi River	....do	493. 11
Quebec, mean high tide in Saint Lawrence River	Canada	15. 37
Rock Island, C., R. I. & P. depot track	Illinois	568. 68
Rock Island, H. W. 1852 Mississippi River	....do	566. 68
Rock Island, city-base	....do	546. 68
Sioux City, R. R. track on levee	Iowa	1, 123 35
Sioux City, bed of Missouri River	....do	1, 094. 00
Sioux City, L. W. Missouri River	....do	1, 104. 00
Saint Joseph, H. W. Missouri River	Missouri	820. 11
Saint Louis, city directrix	....do	428. 29
Saint Louis, H. W. 1844, Mississippi River	....do	435. 87
Saint Louis, H. W. 1858, Mississippi River	....do	431. 57
Saint Louis, H. W. 1851, Mississippi River	....do	431. 17
Saint Louis, L. W. extreme	....do	394. 48
Saint Louis, ord. wa. Mississippi River	....do	408. 00
Saint Louis, center of bridge on R. R. track	....do	485. 80
Saint Louis, center of bridge on wagon-road	....do	510. 04
Steubenville, L. W. in Ohio River	Ohio	630. 77
Terre Haute, T. H. & Ind. depot	Indiana	504. 75
Terre Haute, H. W. in Wabash River	....do	485. 45

*This determination is not checked, and should not be considered of equal quality with the others.

Elevations of points determined in this investigation—Continued.

Names of determined points.	Name of State.	Altitude in feet above the mean surface of the ocean.
Terre Haute, ord. wa. Wabash River	Indiana	467.45
Terre Haute, bed Wabash River	...do	453.95
Three Rivers, mean tide	Canada	15.00
Vincennes, Ind. & V. R. R. depot track	Indiana	434.39
Vincennes, H. W. in Wabash River	...do	425.39
Vincennes, L. W. in Wabash River	...do	413.39
Vandalia, junction of track of St., L. V. & T. H. & Ill. C. R. R	Illinois	511.89

www.ingramcontent.com/pod-product-compliance
Lightning Source LLC
LaVergne TN
LVHW011127110826
845150LV00008B/2271

* 9 7 8 1 4 1 8 1 9 4 8 6 4 *